Topic 1

Business objectives and growth

Sizes and types of firms

This section introduces you to the different types of firm that exist in the economy and why some firms are large, while others remain small. You are also expected to understand the distinction between the public and private sectors, as well as between profit and not-for-profit organisations.

1 Explain what is meant by the 'divorce of ownership and control'. (AO1)
2 marks

2 Outline one difference between a public sector and a private sector organisation. (AO1)
2 marks

3 Are the following reasons why firms remain small or why they grow? Briefly explain your answer.

a To gain economies of scale (AO1, AO2)
2 marks

b To target niche markets (AO1, AO2)
2 marks

Read the following stimulus material and answer the question that follows. The text is similar to the extracts used by Edexcel in the data-response section of the A-level examinations.

Oxfam tweet hits the headlines

Oxfam has hit the headlines due to a twitter message about the current austerity programme implemented by the UK government. The tweet highlighted the rise of food poverty in the country, linking this partially to cuts in benefits that have been implemented. Conservative MP Conor Burns has made a formal complaint about the organisation and has said he could not see 'how using funds donated to charity to campaign politically can be in accord with Oxfam's charitable status'.

4 With reference to the information provided, explain what type of organisation Oxfam is. (AO2, AO3)
3 marks

Business growth

Many firms will look to increase in size either via organic growth (internal) or via takeovers and mergers (external growth), in order to gain benefits, such as higher profits and economies of scale. However, some firms may not be able to gain these benefits as they are unable to grow, due to various constraints, or may suffer difficulties as a result of their growth, such as diseconomies of scale.

The opposite of mergers are demergers — where one firm is split into two separate businesses. This will affect the business itself, as well as consumers and workers. You need to know the reasons why demergers occur and their various impacts too.

5 For each of the following examples, identify the type of business growth that the business is undertaking. Briefly explain your answer.

   a Google, a search engine, taking over YouTube, a music website (AO1, AO2)   `2 marks`

   b Aldi opening more supermarkets in the UK following its recent success (AO1, AO2)   `2 marks`

   c Amazon.com taking over book publishers (AO1, AO2)   `2 marks`

6 Briefly explain two possible:

   a reasons why a firm may undertake a demerger (AO3)   `4 marks`

   b benefits of a demerger for consumers (AO3)   `4 marks`

Read the following stimulus material and answer the questions that follow. The text is similar to the extracts used by Edexcel in the data-response section of the Unit 3 examination.

Casino merger sent to Competition Commission

A takeover involving two of the top three casinos in the UK could be blocked by competition authorities. Rank Group has proposed a takeover of Gala Casinos but it must gain approval from the Competition Commission, after being referred to it by the Office of Fair Trading (OFT). A successful takeover would mean an extra 23 Rank Casinos, potentially making it the UK's largest casino operator.

There are concerns that there would be a lack of competition in the casino market following the move by Rank Group, as there would only be two major national casinos left. The OFT has claimed that this lack of competition, locally and nationally, could leave consumers significantly worse off. The Competition Commission may allow the deal to go ahead if Rank agrees to sell some existing casinos or if it is prevented from buying casinos in areas where little competition exists.

7 Identify and define the type of integration taking place in the UK casino market. (AO1, AO2) `2 marks`

....

....

....

8 To what extent is Rank likely to benefit from its takeover of Gala? (AO3, AO4) `10 marks`

....

....

....

....

....

....

....

....

....

....

....

....

....

....

....

....

....

....

....

9 Discuss whether Rank's takeover of Gala is likely to 'leave consumers significantly worse off'. (AO3, AO4)

8 marks

....
....
....
....
....
....
....
....
....
....

10 Other than the Gala merger possibly being blocked, assess two other possible constraints on future growth that Rank may face. (AO3, AO4)

8 marks

....
....
....
....
....
....
....
....
....
....
....
....

Business objectives

Most economic models assume that firms will maximise profits. However, in some companies, managers may wish to achieve alternative objectives from the owners. Different objectives can be shown diagrammatically.

Figure 1 shows the total revenue and total cost curves for an imperfectly competitive firm.

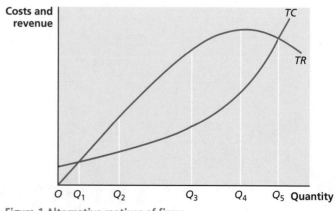

Figure 1 Alternative motives of firms

11 Define the terms 'profit satisficing' and 'profit maximisation'. (AO1) **2 marks**

....

....

....

....

12 How can the 'principal-agent problem' explain managers being able to pursue objectives other than profit maximisation? (AO3) **3 marks**

....

....

....

....

....

....

....

13 With reference to the appropriate quantity in Figure 1, explain one reason why managers may pursue an objective of:

a revenue maximisation (AO2, AO3) **4 marks**

....

....

....

....

....

....

....

....

b sales maximisation (AO2, AO3) **4 marks**

....

....

....

....

....

....

....

....

....

Exam-style questions (multiple choice and short answer)

For multiple-choice questions, circle the letter of the answer that you think is correct.

1 In 2002 eBay, the online auction site, bought PayPal, an online payment company, but in 2014 the company announced a demerger.

⏱ 6

    a Explain why the existence of diseconomies of scale may make it beneficial for eBay and PayPal to demerge. (AO1, AO2, AO3)

4 marks

    b Which type of organisation best describes eBay? (AO1)

1 mark

        A Private sector but not-for-profit

        B Private sector, aiming to make profits

        C Public sector but not for-profit

        D Public sector, aiming to make profits

2 The manager of a chain of high-street book stores is meeting the £10 million profit target of shareholders and is therefore able to pursue objectives other than profit maximisation.

⏱ 6

    a Which of the following best describes the manager's behaviour? (AO1)

1 mark

        A Sales maximisation

        B Demerging

        C Horizontal integration

        D Profit satisficing

    b Explain one constraint on the organic growth of the high-street book store in future. (AO1, AO2, AO3)

4 marks

Exam-style question (data response)

Extract 1: Hotel Chocolat

According to its website, Hotel Chocolat is 'a British chocolatier that encompasses a new type of chocolate company, which connects luxury chocolate making and retailing with cocoa growing — it is one of the world's few chocolate makers to actually grow cocoa'. Hotel Chocolat sells four different chocolate bars in store, all of which are 100% cocoa. The chocolatier, which launched 11 years ago, saw underlying profits jump 144% to £8.3m in the last 6 months of 2014.

Hotel Chocolat is one of many firms looking to benefit from vertically integrating with its supply chain. For example, Morrisons supermarket has taken over many farms which supply its store while Hotel Chocolat grows its own cocoa. This should help these firms control costs.

However, close management of the supply chain can also help to control the quality of supplies used and maintain high levels of customer satisfaction. Morrisons is hoping to gain marketing advantages by advertising its produce as 'farm fresh', while Hotel Chocolat relies on its high-quality brand image to gain a share of the chocolate market.

Hotel Chocolat is not the only chocolate manufacturer looking to exploit the rise in demand for cocoa-based chocolate bars. Willie Cocoa also produces chocolate bars with 100% cocoa content. Moreover, Lindt, a Swiss brand, has bars which contain 99% cocoa, compared to traditional brands like Cadbury's that contain just a quarter.

Willie Harcourt, owner of Willie Cocoa, believes that customers are becoming increasingly discerning, comparing them to wine and cheese connoisseurs. This change in consumer tastes is certainly boosting demand for premium chocolate brands. Getting the right quality of cocoa is therefore of paramount importance. Chocolate bars which come from a single cocoa estate can have a unique flavour and quality. In contrast, those bought in bulk by large manufacturers (often from West Africa) may have high yields and allow the benefits of economies of scale but lack that distinctive taste that brands like Hotel Chocolat achieve.

Market research company Mintel estimates that chocolate sales topped £4 billion in the UK in 2014, which could make even a niche market a source of significant profits.

3 a **With reference to Extract 1, explain one possible reason for the recent profitability of Hotel Chocolat. (AO1, AO2, AO3)**   5 marks 6

....

....

....

....

....

....

....

....

....

....

....

....

b Examine whether backward vertical integration will allow Hotel Chocolat to achieve economic efficiency. (AO1, AO2, AO3, AO4) 8 marks 10

c Discuss why some chocolate manufacturers may continue to operate on a small scale while others aim to grow. (AO1, AO2, AO3, AO4) 12 marks 12

Exam-style question (essay)

4 Virgin is a global conglomerate, operating in diverse markets, ranging from commercial space travel (Virgin Galactic) to cable TV and broadband (Virgin Media).

To what extent would further conglomerate integration be beneficial for firms like Virgin? (AO1, AO2, AO3, AO4)

25 marks **30**

Topic 2

Revenues, costs and profits

Revenue

Revenue is the money a business earns from selling its goods and services. It can be classified in a number of different ways including: marginal, average and total revenue.

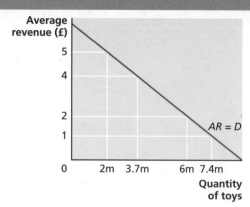

Figure 2 Average revenue for a toy manufacturer with market power

1 Define the term 'marginal revenue'. (AO1) `1 mark`

2 With reference to Figure 2, calculate marginal revenue when the price of toys drops:

a from £5 to £4 (AO2) `3 marks`

b from £2 to £1 (AO2) `3 marks`

3 What is happening to the following as price drops?

a Marginal revenue (AO2) `3 marks`

b Total revenue (AO2) `3 marks`

c Price elasticity of demand (AO2) `3 marks`

④ How would the marginal, average and total revenue curves differ if the firm was operating under perfect competition, such as a wheat farmer? Briefly explain your answer. (AO3)   `5 marks`

....

....

....

....

....

Read the following stimulus material and answer the questions that follow. The text is similar to the extracts used by Edexcel in the data-response section of the A-level examinations.

Loom band craze takes off

Loom bands have become the latest craze with school children across the world. The toy basically comprises small plastic devices that can transform small, colourful rubber bands into home-made jewellery. Sets sell for as little as £1.99 for 1,800.

Sales volumes have exceeded 3 million across the globe, with the toy storming to the top of the most popular toys purchases on Amazon UK, sending revenue for loom band manufacturers skyrocketing. In contrast to traditional product launches that have focused on large-scale TV advertising, loom band sales have taken off through social media, with customers sharing their designs with one another.

Moreover, with major celebrities being seen pictured with loom band jewellery, it is no surprise that the loom band craze has continued to take off. Sales of the bands rose by over 300% following the Duchess of Cambridge being photographed with a red and pink loom bracelet. Other celebrities such as David Beckham, Harry Styles and Miley Cyrus have also been seen showing off their loom bands.

The future of loom bands is by no means certain, however, as fashions come and go. Indeed, some schools are already banning the bands as they have been used by some school children as weapons. The toy market is also notoriously competitive, with new toys released all the time to battle for shelf space in major stores.

⑤ With reference to the extract, explain two reasons why:

a total revenue for loom band manufacturers has been 'skyrocketing' (AO2, AO3)   `4 marks`

....

....

....

....

....

b total revenue for loom bands may fall in future (AO2, AO3)   `4 marks`

....

....

....

....

13

Costs

There are many different costs that affect a business: fixed, variable, marginal, total and average. Here we are considering costs in the short run, i.e. when one factor of production remains fixed.

6 Define the following cost terms:

a marginal cost (AO1)

`1 mark`

b average cost (AO1)

`1 mark`

c fixed costs (AO1)

`1 mark`

7 A small farmer has the following information about his costs. Complete the table. (AO2)

`6 marks`

Total output	TC (£)	TFC (£)	TVC (£)	AVC (£)	AFC (£)	AC (£)	MC (£)
0	100	100		–	–	–	–
3	150			16.67	33.3	50	16.67
10	200						7.14
24	250						3.57
36	300						
40	350						
42	400						

8 Explain the concept of diminishing marginal productivity and the impact it has on marginal cost. (AO3)

`4 marks`

Read the following stimulus material and answer the questions that follow. The text is similar to the extracts used by Edexcel in the data-response section of the A-level examinations.

Warburtons hit by wheat price rise

Wheat prices have risen from $5.50 at the start of the year to $7, mainly due to worries on the supply side. Political instability in Crimea and Ukraine, which together produce 13% of world wheat, has disrupted supply. More concerning are the weather conditions in other major growing regions, such as freezing weather in the USA which has reduced crop yields, as well as drought conditions elsewhere.

This rise in wheat prices is bad news for bread manufacturers, such as Warburtons, along with bakeries, as wheat makes up a significant proportion of their total costs. Consumers may suffer too as prices could rise as a result for wheat-based products like bread and biscuits to compensate for the higher costs.

9 Calculate the percentage increase in the price of wheat since the start of the year. (AO2)   `2 marks`

....

....

10 Is the cost of wheat an example of a variable cost or a fixed cost for Warburtons? Explain your answer. (AO2, AO3)   `3 marks`

....

....

....

11 Illustrate the impact of rising wheat prices on Warburtons' marginal and average cost curves. (AO2, AO3)   `4 marks`

Economies and diseconomies of scale

While short-run costs are explained using the law of diminishing returns, the long-run average cost curve is derived using economies and diseconomies of scale.

You need to know examples of these and be able to apply them to real-world businesses.

12 a What is meant by the term 'minimum efficient scale'? (AO1)   `1 mark`

....

b Illustrate the concept of minimum efficient scale using an appropriate diagram. (AO2)   `3 marks`

13 Using examples, explain what is meant by the terms:

a diseconomies of scale (AO1, AO2)   3 marks

....

....

....

b external economies of scale (AO1, AO2)   3 marks

....

....

....

14 Explain the relationship between the short-run and long-run average cost
curves. (AO3)   3 marks

....

....

....

....

*Read the following stimulus material and answer the questions that follow. The text is similar to the
extracts used by Edexcel in the data-response section of the A-level examinations.*

McDonald's: benefits of growth?

McDonald's is famous all around the world and with over 30,000 restaurants, in over 100 countries,
it is the largest global fast-food operator and a hugely reputable brand. Some of its success
has come through its ability to achieve economies of scale in one form or other. For example,
McDonald's is able to purchase in vast quantities to provide the same menu worldwide, gains
preferential rates from the financial sector and benefits from a large advertising budget that it can
spread over the countless burgers and fries that it sells.

15 Define the term 'purchasing economies of scale'. (AO1)   2 marks

....

....

16 With reference to the information provided or your own knowledge, outline two
other types of economies of scale that McDonald's could gain. (AO1, AO2)   4 marks

....

....

....

....

....

Normal profit, supernormal profit and losses

Profit can be calculated as total revenue minus total cost. Economists also make a distinction between normal and supernormal profits. However, firms can also make losses and you need to be able to explain whether such losses will cause a firm to shut down or remain in business.

17 Define the term 'normal profit'. (AO1)   `1 mark`

....

....

18 A small business has the following costs and revenues. Complete the total revenue and total profit columns in the table below. (AO2)   `2 marks`

Quantity	Price (£)	Total revenue (£)	Total cost (£)	Total profit (£)
150	5		300	
300	4		450	
450	3		600	

19 Figure 3 shows a profit-maximising firm.

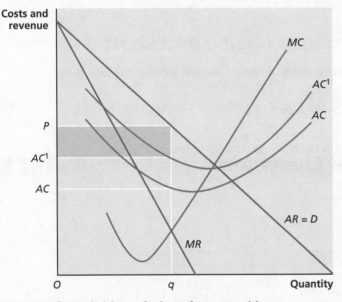

Figure 3 Profit maximising under imperfect competition

a Add the short-run and long-run shut-down points to Figure 3. (AO2)   `2 marks`

b Explain why this firm should remain in business in the short run but shut down in the long run. (AO2, AO3)   `3 marks`

....

....

....

....

....

Read the following stimulus material and answer the question that follows. The text is similar to the extracts used by Edexcel in the data-response section of the A-level examinations.

Airlines forecast profits

World airlines are forecast to gain $12.7bn in profits by the end of the year. Lower oil prices and record passenger numbers are helping to drive up profits for the major global airlines despite a weak economic outlook and low profit margins. Airlines have also started to charge for meals, extra baggage and priority seating; revenue from these services should rise to $36bn (or 5% of total revenue) this year.

20 **Explain two reasons for airlines being 'forecast to gain $12.7bn in profits'. (AO2, AO3)** 4 marks

....

....

....

....

....

....

....

Exam-style questions (multiple choice and short answer)

For multiple-choice questions, circle the letter of the answer that you think is correct.

1 **A US car manufacturer is producing in the short run where marginal cost is positive but falling.** 6

a **Explain what is happening to the US car manufacturer's total cost when marginal cost is positive but falling. (AO1, AO2, AO3)** 4 marks

....

....

....

....

....

....

In the long run the car manufacturer decides to build a second factory.

b **If the car manufacturer has increased output beyond its minimum efficient scale, which of the following best describes its situation? (AO1)** 1 mark

    A Falling long-run average cost

    B External economies of scale

    C Diseconomies of scale

    D Internal economies of scale

2 The table below shows the revenue for a local hairdresser.

Quantity	Average revenue (£)	Total revenue (£)
10	15	150
20	13	260
30	11	330

If the hairdresser decides to drop its price from £13 to £11:

a Calculate the marginal revenue. You are advised to show your workings. (AO2)

b Calculate the price elasticity of demand. You are advised to show your workings. (AO2)

c The hairdresser's average revenue is currently below average cost but above average variable cost. This implies it: (AO1)   1 mark

A Will remain in business in the short run

B Is unable to make a contribution to paying back total fixed costs

C Is currently making normal profits

D Will have to shut down immediately

Economic efficiency

Economic efficiency is a central concept in Theme 3 and needs to be assessed when considering different market structures. Efficiency can be assessed using diagrammatical analysis, such as of perfect competition, as we will see in the next section, or by looking at case study material for certain real-life cases, such as Network Rail.

---

1 Define the term 'dynamic efficiency'. (AO1)   `1 mark`

2 Distinguish between productive and allocative efficiency. (AO1)   `2 marks`

Read the following stimulus material and answer the questions that follow. The text is similar to the extracts used by Edexcel in the data-response section of the A-level examinations.

Network Rail forced to cut costs

Network Rail is the only firm in charge of the UK's rail infrastructure, making it a pure monopoly. There are often worries that monopolies could suffer from x-inefficiency. Indeed, the railways regulator has estimated that the cost of running the rail network until 2019 should be £2 billion lower than the figure estimated by Network Rail.

The regulator has therefore told Network Rail that it will need to cut costs by £2 billion over the next 5 years. However, these cost reductions must be achieved while maintaining a reliable service for train customers, with a target of 92.5% of punctual train journeys.

3 With reference to Network Rail, explain what is meant by 'x-inefficiency'. (AO2, AO3)   `3 marks`

4 Why may attempts by Network Rail to improve productive efficiency reduce its allocative efficiency? (AO3)   `4 marks`

Perfect competition

Perfect competition is a market structure at the opposite end of the spectrum to monopoly. There are very few (if any) perfectly competitive markets, as the assumptions behind the model are fairly strict. However, it is a useful comparison point for other market structures in terms of economic efficiency, for example.

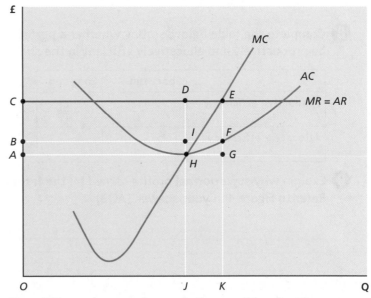

Figure 4 Costs and revenues for a perfectly competitive wheat farm

---

5 Explain what is meant by a 'price-taking firm'. (AO1)   1 mark

....

....

....

....

6 Other than price taking, list three assumptions of the perfect competition model. (AO1)   3 marks

....

....

....

....

....

....

7 Figure 4 shows a small profit-maximising wheat farm aiming to maximise profit. Which letter(s) represent the following in the short run? (AO2)

a Profit-maximising quantity and price   2 marks

....

b Total revenue   1 mark

....

c Total costs   1 mark

....

d Supernormal profit/loss area   2 marks

....

8 Complete the table below, stating whether a perfectly competitive firm will be productively and allocatively efficient in the short and long run. (AO2)   `4 marks`

	Short run	Long run
Productive efficiency		
Allocative efficiency		

9 Explain why supernormal profits earned by the farm will fall in the long run. Refer to Figure 4 in your answer. (AO3)   `6 marks`

....

....

....

....

....

....

....

....

Read the following stimulus material and answer the questions that follow. The text is similar to the extracts used by Edexcel in the data-response section of the A-level examinations.

The steel industry

Steel is one of the most important raw materials bought worldwide and is being increasingly used by China as its economy expands. However, steelmakers are currently making wafer-thin profits, especially in Europe. Some commentators have suggested that this is unsurprising as the steel industry is near to perfect competition. Despite market leader ArcelorMittal having 6% of global market share, there are many firms in the market. Indeed, 60 firms currently produce over 5 million tonnes or more, most of which is produced to an industry standard.

10 Outline two reasons why the steel industry could be considered 'near to perfect competition'. (AO2, AO3)   `4 marks`

....

....

....

....

....

....

11 Explain why perfectly competitive firms are always allocatively efficient. (AO3)   `3 marks`

....

....

....

....

Monopolistic competition

Monopolistic competition is commonly confused with monopoly by many students, but as a market structure it is nearest to perfect competition. As with other market structures you need to know the assumptions behind it, and be able to model it diagrammatically (in the short and long run) and assess its economic efficiency.

12 Identify one assumption in monopolistic competition that is different from:

a   perfect competition (AO1)   `1 mark`

b   pure monopoly (AO1)   `1 mark`

13 State two real-life markets which closely resemble monopolistic competition. (AO2)   `2 marks`

14 Using an appropriate costs and revenue diagram, illustrate the long-run equilibrium for a profit-maximising firm operating in a monopolistically competitive market. (AO3)   `3 marks`

15 Annotating your diagram above to illustrate your answer, explain whether the firm is:

a   productively efficient (AO2)   `2 marks`

b   allocatively efficient (AO2)   `2 marks`

16 With reference to the assumptions of monopolistic competition, explain why monopolistically competitive firms:

a   face a downward-sloping demand curve (AO3)

3 marks

....

....

....

b   only make normal profits in the long run (AO3)

3 marks

....

....

....

Read the following stimulus material and answer the question that follows. The text is similar to the extracts used by Edexcel in the data-response section of the A-level examinations.

Taxi industry struggles?

The taxi industry is a highly competitive market in the UK, with no firms having a dominant market share. In fact, there are over 18,000 taxi firms in the country, employing nearly 300,000 people.

In order to survive in such an industry, taxis must try to differentiate themselves in some way. This could be done through superior customer service, more comfortable vehicles and quicker response times. Some go further to find a gap in the market, such as Pink Taxis, which are driven by women and take exclusively women passengers.

However, over the last 5 years the industry has been hit hard by the financial crisis, when low consumer confidence and falling tourist numbers reduced profitability and many firms left the market. The challenge for many other taxi companies continues.

17 To what extent is the UK taxi industry a good example of monopolistic competition? (AO2, AO3, AO4)

8 marks

....

....

....

....

....

....

....

....

....

....

....

....

....

....

....

....

Oligopoly

Oligopolies are the most common real-life markets. They can be modelled using game theory. Many of the industries we use on a day-to-day basis have the key features of an oligopoly, such as cinemas, high-street banking and mobile networks. Firms in these markets will often compete with each other, for example by developing new products or using other marketing techniques.

However, there is also an incentive to collude together and restrict competition, either overtly or tacitly. This is illegal and firms suspected of colluding will be investigated by the competition authorities and sanctions put in place.

Figure 5 shows information regarding the UK accountancy market.

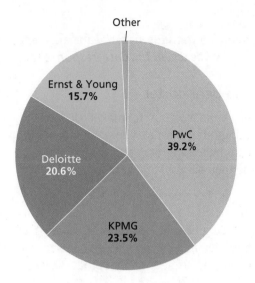

Figure 5 Market share of the 'big four' accountancy firms

---

18 With reference to the UK accountancy industry, explain what is meant by a 'four-firm concentration ratio'. (AO1, AO2)   `2 marks`

....

....

....

19 With reference to the UK accountancy industry, explain one characteristic of oligopolistic markets. (AO2, AO3)   `3 marks`

....

....

....

....

....

....

20 Outline one difference between:

a tacit and overt collusion (AO1)   `2 marks`

....

....

....

....

b predatory pricing and limit pricing (AO1)   `2 marks`

....

....

....

Read the following stimulus material and answer the questions that follow. The text is similar to the extracts used by Edexcel in the data-response section of the A-level examinations.

German beer cartel

In 2014, Anheuser Busch (maker of Becks) gave information to the competition authorities implicating other German beer companies for operating as a cartel. This involved the major beer producers increasing prices of draft beer in the range of 5 to 7 euros per hectolitre in order to increase their supernormal profits.

The German beer market is highly concentrated with high barriers to entry. It is full of well-known, reputable brands, and there are significant start-up, distribution and development costs of making and producing beer in Germany. Moreover, beer in Germany is subject to purity laws which limit the number of ingredients that can be used to manufacture the product. While this does not make beer homogeneous, it does limit product differentiation.

The companies involved in the alleged cartel were all well-known brands in the German beer market, including Bitburger, Krombacher, Veltins, Warsteiner and Ernst Barre. Other firms are also suspected of being involved, including Danish company Carlsberg, which is under investigation.

21 Using a simple game theory matrix in your answer, explain two reasons why collusion may have occurred in the German beer market. (AO2, AO3)   `6 marks`

22 Assess one pricing and one non-pricing strategy that German beer manufacturers could use to compete following the end of the cartel. (AO3, AO4)   `10 marks`

Monopoly

At the other extreme on the spectrum of competition is the market structure of monopoly. In theory, a pure monopoly will have 100% market share. Again, this market structure is seen more in theory than in practice but clearly demonstrates the impact on price, quantity, profit and efficiency when a firm totally monopolises a market.

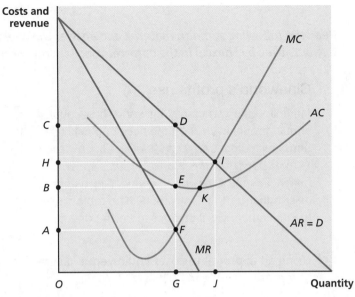

Figure 6 Costs and revenues for a monopoly

23 Define the terms 'natural monopoly' and 'pure monopoly'. (AO1) `2 marks`

24 Figure 6 shows a profit-maximising monopolist earning supernormal profits. Which letter(s) represent the following?

a Profit-maximising price and quantity (AO2) `2 marks`

b Supernormal profit (AO2) `1 mark`

25 With clear reference to Figure 6, explain why the monopolist is both allocatively and productively inefficient. (AO2) `4 marks`

26 Explain one benefit for consumers and one benefit for employees of a firm having significant monopoly power. (AO3) `4 marks`

Read the following stimulus material and answer the questions that follow. The text is similar to the extracts used by Edexcel in the data-response section of the A-level examinations.

Cineworld's profits rise

Multiplex, the owner of Cineworld, has doubled annual profits in 2015 on the back of blockbuster films including *The Lego Movie, Inbetweeners 2* and *Dawn of the Planet of the Apes*. Like many cinemas, Cineworld continues to use price discrimination to boost profits. The table shows the different prices it charges in north London.

	Before 5pm weekdays	After 5pm weekdays	Weekends
Adults	£8.60	£9.70	£9.70
Students	£7.10	£7.10	£7.10

27 Using an appropriate costs and revenue diagram, explain why Cineworld saw profits double in 2015. (AO2, AO3)

4 marks

....
....
....
....
....
....
....
....
....
....
....
....

28 With reference to Figure 6, discuss the likely effectiveness of price discrimination as a method of increasing profits for Cineworld. (AO3, AO4)

8 marks

....
....
....
....
....
....
....
....
....
....
....

Monopsony

When studying a pure monopoly the emphasis was on there being only one seller in the market, for example Network Rail. In contrast, monopsony power is related to powerful buyers, not sellers, and the use of this power to improve their profitability. Supermarkets are good examples of firms with monopsony power, such as Tesco using its position to exploit its suppliers.

㉙ What is the difference between a 'pure monopsony' and a 'pure monopoly'? (AO1)   `2 marks`

....

....

㉚ A computer manufacturer has significant monopsony power over its component suppliers. Explain the effect on the manufacturer's monopsony power of:

a component suppliers integrating horizontally (AO3)   `3 marks`

....

....

b lower market concentration among component suppliers (AO1, AO2)   `3 marks`

....

....

Read the following stimulus material and answer the questions that follow. The text is similar to the extracts used by Edexcel in the data-response section of the A-level examinations.

Mega-dairies aim to challenge supermarkets

Complaints from dairy farmers against powerful supermarkets are nothing new. In 2007–08 it was reported that farmers on average made a loss of 1p on every pint sold and now many farmers are paid below the cost of production. Supermarkets can use their considerable buying power to keep the cost of milk low, in order to keep prices competitive for consumers. Morrisons has responded to critics by offering a new milk brand that will mean farmers are paid 10p more per litre.

However, some dairy farmers have decided to increase their scale in order to survive and have therefore created mega-dairies. Nocton in Lincolnshire is the site of the UK's first mega-dairy, a concept that has been operating in the USA for many years. A mega-dairy is typically 30 times bigger than a normal dairy farm, with cows housed indoors in massive warehouses. The hope is that mega-dairies will allow dairy farmers to survive as they can achieve lower costs through economies of scale, as well as giving them more power at the bargaining table when negotiating with the supermarkets.

㉛ Define the term 'monopsony power'. (AO1)   `2 marks`

....

㉜ Analyse two benefits to customers of supermarkets' monopsony power. (AO3, AO4)   `6 marks`

....

....

....

....

....

33 Examine the likely negative impacts on UK dairy farmers of supermarkets' monopsony power. (AO3, AO4)

`10 marks`

....

....

....

....

....

....

....

....

....

....

....

....

Contestability

When studying topics like monopoly and perfect competition earlier in the course, we tended to make the assumption that if we know the market structure, we can discern the conduct and performance of an industry. However, in a contestable market with the threat of competition, a monopolist may have to adapt its behaviour.

34 Using examples, explain the term 'sunk cost'. (AO1, AO2)

`3 marks`

....

....

....

35 With reference to the pharmaceutical industry, analyse why the following are significant barriers to entry:

a   economies of scale (AO2, AO3)

`3 marks`

....

....

....

b   brand loyalty (AO2, AO3)

`3 marks`

....

....

....

c patents (AO2, AO3) 3 marks

....

....

....

36 Explain the likely impact on a firm's pricing of its market becoming more contestable. (AO3) 4 marks

....

....

....

....

Read the following stimulus material and answer the questions that follow. The text is similar to the extracts used by Edexcel in the data-response section of the A-level examinations.

Mobile phone apps

It is estimated that in 2015, over 180 billion smartphone apps will be downloaded, with over 1.5 million apps available on both the Apple App Store and Google Play. Every week over 15,000 new apps are launched, as firms take advantage of the relatively low entry costs. Apps make programs that were once only available on PCs available to smartphone users too. They include programs such as Facebook, streaming radio and, of course, the game Angry Birds.

However, revenue gained from apps is concentrated among a few developers. In the USA, for example, 25 developers accounted for half of all app revenue, most of these being gaming apps from well-known brands such as Electronic Arts and Disney.

37 Define the term 'contestable market'. (AO1) 2 marks

....

....

....

38 To what extent is the mobile app industry contestable? (AO3, AO4) 10 marks

....

....

....

....

....

....

....

....

....

....

....

....

....

....

Exam-style questions (multiple choice and short answer)

For multiple-choice questions, circle the letter of the answer that you think is correct.

1 Figure 7 shows the costs and revenues for a small corn farmer operating under the conditions of perfect competition.

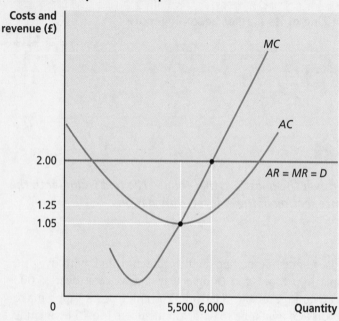

Figure 7

a Calculate the supernormal profit made by an individual farm in the short run. You are advised to show your workings. (AO2)

2 marks

b Calculate the total revenue made by an individual farm in the long run. You are advised to show your workings. (AO2)

2 marks

c Which of the following statements is true in both perfect competition and monopolistic competition? (AO1)

1 mark

A Productive inefficiency in the short run

B Firms able to use price discrimination

C High market concentration

D Allocative efficiency in the long run

2 Fizz and Sparkli are two cola drink manufacturers operating in a duopoly and their profits are shown in the game theory matrix below.

	Sparkli sets £1.50	Sparkli sets £1
Fizz sets £1.50	Both earn £300m	Fizz earns £90m Sparkli earns £360m
Fizz sets £1	Fizz earns £360m Sparkli earns £90m	Both earn £200

a   Fizz and Sparkli are currently setting their price at £1. If both firms colluded at £1.50, they would both see their profits increase by: (AO1)   1 mark

   A   £50 million

   B   £100 million

   C   £150 million

   D   £300 million

b   Calculate the ratio of profits between the two firms if Fizz lowered its price back to £1. Show your answer in its simplest form. (AO2)   2 marks

....

....

c   Explain one reason why a collusive agreement between the two firms to price at £1.50 may break down. (AO1, AO3)   2 marks

....

....

....

3 Forbes.com reported that it costs on average $4 billion to develop a new pharmaceutical drug, with some drugs requiring up to $11 billion.   ⏱ 6

a   This implies the pharmaceutical industry is likely to have low: (AO1)   1 mark

   A   Concentration

   B   Contestability

   C   Sunk costs

   D   Levels of regulation

Figure 8 shows the costs and revenues for a profit-maximising pharmaceutical firm.

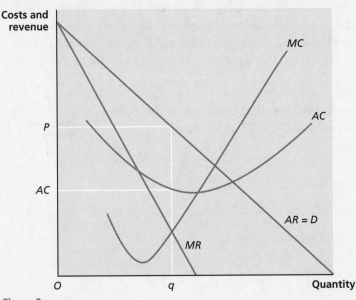

Figure 8

b   Annotate the diagram to show the impact of increased spending on research and development on the firm's cost curves and profits. (AO1)   2 marks

c Explain one possible barrier to entry in the pharmaceutical industry. (AO1) (AO2)

2 marks

....

....

....

Exam-style question (data response)

Extract 1: Apple fixed e-book prices

The US Department for Justice has found that Apple has conspired with five publishers to fix the price of electronic books (or e-books). Prosecutors estimate that the higher prices could have cost customers hundreds of millions of dollars. It is reported that the main evidence used to convict Apple was a combination of internal e-mails sent by Apple's senior vice president, Eddy Cue, to the publishers involved, and transcripts from the late Steve Jobs' biographer.

Extract 2: Amazon's monopsony power

Amazon is a powerful buyer and has significant market power over publishers. Amazon sells 9 out of 10 e-books in the UK and when it comes to negotiations, it is certainly in a strong position. In recent times Amazon has forced publishers into significant discounts for the e-books they sell to the site, and it is now forcing British publishers to cover the cost of the VAT charge on e-book sales, currently at 20%. In many cases this can leave e-book publishers with as little as 10% of the price paid by Amazon's customers online. Publishers who step out of line can quickly be replaced by others.

Some argue that Amazon may have helped the e-book market avoid suffering the same fate as online music, where piracy has hit profits substantially. Others worry that Amazon's monopsony power will force smaller publishers out of business and reduce consumer choice of books and authors.

However, Amazon recorded a $214m loss in 2014. The company has therefore tried to diversify away from just distributing and selling gadgets, to providing a broader range of digital services. In recent months, the top 10 selling items worldwide were all digital products, including the Kindle range as well as other digital content. This could explain the surprise rise in profits to $92m for the 3 months to 30 June 2015.

4 a **With reference to Extract 1, examine the view that collusion in the e-book market will reduce economic efficiency. (AO1, AO2, AO3, AO4)**

8 marks 10

....

....

....

....

....

....

....

....

2 marks

b   Assess the possible economic effects of Amazon's monopsony power in
    the e-book market. (AO1, AO2, AO3, AO4)   10 marks   12

....

....

....

....

....

....

....

....

c   Other than by exploiting its monopsony power, discuss the possible
    strategies Amazon could use to increase its profitability. Use game
    theory to support your answer. (AO1, AO2, AO3, AO4)   15 marks   18

....

....

....

....

....

....

....

....

....

....

....

....

....

....

....

....

....

....

b   Assess the possible economic effects of Amazon's monopsony power in
    the e-book market. (AO1, AO2, AO3, AO4)   10 marks   12

....

Topic 4

Labour market

Demand and supply of labour

The demand and supply curves that were studied in Theme 1 now need to be applied to labour markets. You need to understand the factors that determine demand and supply for different occupations, such as for UK builders.

1 Using the example of builders, explain what is meant by derived demand. (AO1, AO2)   **2 marks**

....

....

2 Explain two factors that will influence the supply of labour for builders in the UK. (AO2, AO3)   **4 marks**

....

....

....

....

Wage determination

Putting the demand and supply of labour together allows the equilibrium wage to be determined for a particular occupation. You need to be able to determine the equilibrium wage in both competitive labour markets and imperfectly competitive labour markets, such as where there are employers with monopsony power.

Figure 9 shows an imperfectly competitive labour market, with a monopsonist employer setting wage equal to W_2.

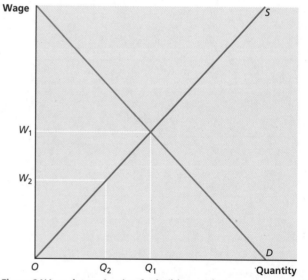

Figure 9 Wage determination for builders with a monopsony employer

3 With reference to Figure 9, briefly explain the impact of a monopsony employer on:

a builders' wages (AO1, AO2)   **3 marks**

....

....

b number of builders employed (AO1, AO2)   `3 marks`

....

....

....

Read the following stimulus material and answer the questions that follow. The text is similar to the extracts used by Edexcel in the data-response section of the A-level examinations.

Australian miners see pay rise as iron-ore price booms

Workers in the Australian mining sector are the best paid in the economy and continue to see their incomes rise significantly, by around 4–5% each year. This continued rise in earnings comes as a direct result of rising demand for commodities, such as iron ore, which Australia mines and exports. For example, Western Australia recently announced it will need 10,000 new workers for its Roy Hill iron-ore mine but the supply of miners is likely to be inelastic in the short run.

The Australian government is worried about the rapidly rising wages in the commodity sector and is taking action to boost future labour supply. Measures it is considering include retraining workers via adult apprenticeship programmes and encouraging skilled immigrants by fast-tracking visas. However, with lower commodity prices in 2015 hitting Australian mines these measures may not be necessary.

4 Explain one reason why 'the supply of miners is likely to be inelastic in the short run'. (AO2, AO3)   `3 marks`

....

....

....

....

5 With reference to the information provided, discuss why miners' wages rose in Australia. Illustrate your answer with a demand and supply diagram. (AO3, AO4)   `8 marks`

....

....

....

....

....

....

....

....

....

....

....

....

....

Labour market failure and government intervention

As we saw in Theme 1, markets can fail and this is also true for labour markets. Therefore there can be a need for government intervention, such as when there is labour immobility or when a monopsony employer is exploiting workers. You need to be able to assess the effectiveness of these policies at solving labour market failure.

6 Explain why geographic immobility of labour can cause market failure in the labour market. (AO2, AO3) **4 marks**

....

....

....

....

7 Complete the table below by stating one possible cause and an appropriate government intervention for geographic and occupational immobility. (AO1, AO2) **4 marks**

Type of immobility	Possible cause	Government intervention
Geographic immobility		
Occupational immobility		

8 Using a demand and supply diagram, illustrate how the national minimum wage can cause unemployment in a competitive labour market. (AO3) **4 marks**

Read the following stimulus material and answer the questions that follow. The text is similar to the extracts used by Edexcel in the data-response section of the A-level examinations.

Public sector vs private sector wages

In July 2014, hundreds of thousands of public sector workers took part in strikes, including teachers, firefighters and council workers. One of the main issues is public sector wage setting. In 2010 there was a freeze in public sector pay and since 2012 the salary rises have been capped at 1% in nominal terms, but this has still meant real wage cuts for workers due to inflation being over 3% at the time. This fall in living standards has led to unions taking action to try to improve conditions for their members. At least inflation has now fallen to near 0%, helping boost real incomes for the public sector.

However, in some private sector industries there are concerns at the other end of the income distribution, i.e. that the top earners are over-paid. Research has shown that executive pay is now over 150 times that of the average worker, up from just over 50 a few years ago. Some firms have voluntarily capped this ratio, such as John Lewis and TSB, but there have been calls for the government to introduce maximum wages to fight such inequality.

9 With reference to examples in the extract, explain what is meant by:

a 'public sector wage setting' (AO1, AO2) `3 marks`

b 'real wage cuts' (AO1, AO2) `3 marks`

10 Assess the likely economic effects of the UK government introducing a maximum wage. Illustrate your answer with an appropriate diagram. (AO3, AO4) `8 marks`

Exam-style questions (multiple choice and short answer)

For multiple-choice questions, circle the letter of the answer that you think is correct.

1 In August 2015 the very last deep pit coal mine in the UK closed, meaning hundreds of workers may need to find alternative employment. However, there is an issue with labour mobility for many coal miners. ⏲ 6

    a Which of the following will determine the occupational mobility of coal miners? (AO1) `1 mark`

        A Regional house price differences

        B Family ties to the local area

        C The level of transferable skills of miners

        D Differences in costs of living between areas

    b Outline one policy that the UK government could implement to improve:

        i the occupational mobility of UK coal miners (AO1, AO3) `2 marks`

        ii the geographic mobility of UK coal miners (AO1, AO3) `2 marks`

2 Over 1 million of Britain's lowest-paid workers are set to benefit from new national minimum wage rates introduced in October 2014. The rate rise to £6.50 per hour is the first real terms increase in the minimum wage since 2008. ⏲ 6

    a The most likely rationale for the increase in the national minimum wage is to reduce: (AO1) `1 mark`

        A Real wage rates

        B Costs for small businesses

        C Income inequality

        D Employment in low-skill industries

    b Explain what is meant by a 'real terms increase in the minimum wage'. (AO1) `2 marks`

    c Explain why an increase in the national minimum wage could leave wage levels unchanged for higher-paid earners. (AO1, AO3) `2 marks`

Exam-style question (data response)

Extract 1: Chancellor clashes with EU over cap on banker bonuses

George Osborne has withdrawn the UK's legal challenge to the EU cap on banker bonuses. The cap restricts bonuses to 100% of bankers' pay or 200% with shareholder approval. The cap is designed to reduce incentives for bankers to take excessive risks in order to gain short-term rewards, as seen in the run-up to the financial crisis.

However, the Treasury claims it will just push up basic pay and these higher costs may be harder to reduce during lower performing years, while also driving talent away from Europe. The chancellor said: 'the fact remains these are badly designed rules that are pushing up bankers' pay not reducing it. These rules may be legal but they are entirely self-defeating, so we need to find another way to end rewards for failure in our banks.' Indeed, there is still no limit on the total remuneration a banker can receive. These concerns were echoed by governor of the Bank of England, Mark Carney. One alternative could be a cap on total annual remuneration a banker receives, including their salary and bonuses.

3 a Explain why the EU bonus cap will still mean there is 'no limit on the total remuneration a banker can receive'. (AO1, AO2, AO3) `5 marks` `6`

....
....
....
....
....
....

b Examine the arguments against imposing a maximum level for the total annual remuneration a banker can receive. (AO1, AO2, AO3, AO4) `8 marks` `10`

....
....
....
....
....
....
....
....
....
....
....
....
....
....

Topic 5

Controlling monopolies and mergers

Monopolies could exploit their market power and damage the public interest. Therefore, policymakers need to control the growth of firms via mergers and introducing regulations in key industries, such as OFWAT for water. However, this is not without limitations, such as the problems of regulatory capture and imperfect information.

1 Explain one reason why competition authorities may not allow a merger to go ahead. (AO3)
`3 marks`

2 Analyse one type of regulation that OFWAT could use to improve the economic efficiency of UK water providers. (AO2, AO3)
`3 marks`

Read the following stimulus material and answer the question that follows. The text is similar to the extracts used by Edexcel in the data-response section of the A-level examinations.

Rail regulations

Regulated rail fares are set to rise in the UK for another year, with prices increasing on average by 3.9% in England, Wales and Scotland. Regulated fares are currently calculated using an 'RPI + K' formula, where prices can rise by inflation plus an additional amount for investment in the rail network. The hope is that this long-term investment will reduce the cost of running the railways and allow better service for passengers, as well as a return to lower fares. However, with prices rising and real incomes stagnating, questions are being asked about the current regulatory system. This comes at a time when the Office of Rail Regulation announced that Network Rail missed all its performance targets for punctuality in England and Wales, although it praised improvements in Scotland where targets were met.

3 With reference to the extract and your own economic knowledge, assess the view that current UK rail regulations are effective. (AO3, AO4)
`10 marks`

Plan your answer here and complete on additional paper.

Promoting competition and contestability

Greater competition and contestability in markets can help improve consumer welfare, as firms are forced to compete on price, as well as in terms of quality and choice. Policymakers can therefore implement various methods to gain such benefits of contestability and competition.

4 **Briefly explain how the following policies could increase competition in markets:**

a **promoting small business (AO3)** `2 marks`

....

....

b **competitive tendering (AO3)** `2 marks`

....

....

Read the following stimulus material and answer the question that follows. The text is similar to the extracts used by Edexcel in the data-response section of the A-level examinations.

Royal Mail privatisation

In 2013, the government privatised the Royal Mail by floating shares on the stock market. The main reason for the privatisation was to give Royal Mail access to private sector investment to allow it to grow and compete. However, unions argue privatisation will lead to a drop in service, with a universal postal service under threat, and could harm working conditions.

The extra finance could be used to expand Royal Mail's parcel delivery service to meet demand from internet shopping and compete with new rivals, such as TNT and UK Mail, which joined the market following deregulation in 2006. Deregulation meant that Royal Mail lost its position as the monopoly provider and that any licensed operator was able to deliver mail to business and residential customers from 1 January 2006.

5 **Evaluate the possible benefits of one method of government intervention implemented in the postal delivery market mentioned in the extract. (AO3, AO4)** `8 marks`

....

....

....

....

....

....

....

....

....

....

....

....

....

Protecting employees and suppliers

Here we are concerned with government intervention aimed at protecting employees and suppliers rather than consumers. This includes methods to try to prevent the abuse of monopsony power, which can impact on workers (in labour markets) and suppliers (in product markets).

6 **a** **What is meant by the term 'nationalisation'? (AO1)** `1 mark`

....

....

b **Explain one possible benefit of nationalising the UK renewable energy industry. (AO2, AO3)** `3 marks`

....

....

....

....

Read the following stimulus material and answer the question that follows. The text is similar to the extracts used by Edexcel in the data-response section of the A-level examinations.

Hitting back at monopsony

In labour markets the monopsony power of employers has to some extent been tackled by increases in the national minimum wage, although pushing this towards the living wage could do more for low-paid workers.

However, what about suppliers who complain about the same practices in product markets? A group of MPs believe large fines need to be imposed on large supermarkets if they are found guilty of exploiting any of their suppliers. The power to do this would go to Christine Tacon, the groceries code adjudicator, a position created to investigate big supermarkets' practices when dealing with farming suppliers.

Another suggestion is the grouping of farmers into producer organisations. This would hopefully offset the monopsony power of major retailers and improve suppliers' negotiating power.

7 **With reference to the information provided, explain two methods of restricting the monopsony power of firms. (AO2, AO3)** `6 marks`

....

....

....

....

....

....

....

....

....

....

....

The impact of government intervention

The Competition and Markets Authority and regulators, such as OFGEM, implement a variety of policies in order to promote competition and the public interest. You need to be able to analyse the impact of all these policies on:

- prices
- profits
- efficiency
- quality
- choice

However, these government interventions are not without limitations and the policy may not reduce prices or improve choice as desired. For example, policymakers face asymmetric information and regulatory capture.

---

8 Explain why the presence of regulatory capture could limit the effectiveness of government intervention. (AO3) `3 marks`

....

....

....

....

9 a Define the term 'asymmetric information'. (AO1) `2 marks`

....

....

b Explain why asymmetric information may reduce the effectiveness of the Competition and Markets Authority in preventing collusion. (AO3) `6 marks`

....

....

....

....

....

....

....

Exam-style questions (multiple choice and short answer)

For multiple-choice questions, circle the letter of the answer that you think is correct.

1 In 2013 competition authorities allowed Penguin and Random House to complete a £2.4bn merger to create the biggest book publisher in the world. `6`

a Explain how allowing the merger could restrict the monopsony power enjoyed by buyers such as Amazon. (AO1, AO2, AO3) `4 marks`

....

....

....

....

....

b Which of the following could limit the effectiveness of UK competition authorities' ability to control mergers? (AO1)

  A The divorce of ownership and control

  B Asymmetric information

  C UK and EU competition policy being brought into line

  D A lack of regulatory capture

2 The BBC is currently a public sector organisation but prefers to use competitive tendering for projects over £50,000.

  a Which of the following is the most likely reason why the BBC prefers to use competitive tendering? (AO1)

    A The possibility of lower-cost bids when many private firms are involved

    B Private firms should be able to access cheaper finance than the BBC

    C Better pay for workers who win the contract

    D The likelihood of private firms colluding during the tendering process

  b Explain one potential benefit of privatising the BBC. (AO1, AO2, AO3)

Exam-style question (data response)

Extract 1: Are Dover–Calais crossings anti-competitive?

The Competition and Markets Authority (CMA) has finished investigating the cross-Channel ferry market between Dover and Calais. There were concerns that the market may be anti-competitive, resulting in higher prices for passengers and freight firms when crossing the Channel.

Issues had arisen because Eurotunnel, the Channel tunnel operator, also operated ferry crossings. Its company, MyFerryLink, ran 16 crossings a day, in competition with P&O and DFDS. MyFerryLink had previously purchased three ships, from the now liquidated SeaFrance, to prevent DFDS buying them. Eurotunnel's purchase of the ferries meant it had more than half the market and this share could rise in future.

The CMA ruled that having two independent ferry companies competing with the tunnel would be more in the public interest, and it therefore forced the sale of MyFerryLink by Eurotunnel. There was also a concern that should one of the remaining ferry companies shut down, this would leave MyFerryLink having only one ferry operator in competition with it, along with the Channel tunnel.

P&O and DFDS welcomed the move from the competition authorities, believing it would bring fairer competition. P&O claimed that it would reduce the market power of Eurotunnel and that the primary reason why MyFerryLink had gained such a large share was because it had been selling its services below cost. However, Eurotunnel argued that removing a competitor would create a duopoly in the sector and see prices for consumers rise.

3 a   Explain one reason why the Competition and Markets Authority's intervention should lead to a more competitive market for cross-Channel ferries. (AO1, AO2, AO3)

5 marks   6

....

....

....

....

b   Discuss the potential benefits of increased competition in the cross-Channel ferry market as a result of the Competition and Market Authority's intervention. (AO1, AO2, AO3, AO4)

12 marks   14

....

....

....

....

....

....

....

....

....

....

....

....

....

....

Exam-style question (essay)

4   Assess the methods policymakers could use to increase economic efficiency in UK industries. (AO1, AO2, AO3, AO4)

25 marks   30

....

....

....

....

....

....

....

....

(Answer lines continued on p. 48)

Philip Allan, an imprint of Hodder Education, an Hachette UK company,
Blenheim Court, George Street, Banbury, Oxfordshire OX16 5BH

Orders

Bookpoint Ltd, 130 Park Drive, Milton Park, Abingdon, Oxfordshire OX14 4SB

tel: 01235 827827

fax: 01235 400401

e-mail: education@bookpoint.co.uk

Lines are open 9.00 a.m.–5.00 p.m., Monday to Saturday, with a 24-hour
message answering service.

You can also order through the Hodder Education website:
www.hoddereducation.co.uk

© Peter Davis 2016

ISBN 978-1-4718-4459-1

First printed 2016

Impression number   5   4

Year   2020   2019   2018

This guide has been written specifically to support students preparing for
the Edexcel A-level Economics examinations. The content has been neither
approved nor endorsed by Edexcel and remains the sole responsibility of
the authors.

Typeset by Aptara

Printed in Dubai

Hachette UK's policy is to use papers that are natural, renewable and
recyclable products and made from wood grown in sustainable forests.
The logging and manufacturing processes are expected to conform to the
environmental regulations of the country of origin.

ISBN 978-1-4718-4459-1